The Little Plays of Ford Maddox Ford

The following pieces in dramatic form were published, viz., "Perseverance d' Amour" and "The Face of the Night," in the volume bearing the latter name; the "Mother" appeared also in the Fortnightly Review. "King Cophetua" and the "Masque" were published in "Poems for Pictures." I have grouped them here together for the convenience of the reader who does not like poems in dialogue.

Ford Madox Ford was born Ford Hermann Hueffer on 17th December 1873 in Wimbledon, London, England.

Today he is best known for one book, 'The Good Soldier', which is regularly held to be one of the 100 greatest novels of all time. But, rather unfairly, the breadth of his career has been overshadowed. He wrote novels as well as essays, poetry, memoirs and literary criticism. Today he is well-regarded but known only for a few works rather than the grand arc of his career.

Ford collaborated with Joseph Conrad on three novels but would later complain that, as with all his collaborators, and those he so readily championed, his contribution was overshadowed by theirs.

He founded The English Review and The Transatlantic Review which were instrumental in publishing and promoting the works of so many authors and movements.

During WWI he initially worked on propaganda books before enlisting. Ford was invalided back to Britain in 1917, remaining in the army and giving lectures until the War's end. After a spell recuperating in the Sussex countryside he lived mostly in France during the 1920s.

He published the series of four novels known as Parade's End, between 1924 and 1928. These were particularly well-received in America, where Ford spent much of his time from the later 1920s to his death in 1939.

His last years were spent teaching at Olivet College in Olivet, Michigan.

Ford Madox Ford died on 26th June 1939 at Deauville, France at the age of 65.

Index of Contents

TIME.—Thirteenth Century.

PLACE.—In and near the City of Paris.

DRAMATIS PERSONAE—
Anseau dit le Tourangeau, Jeweller to the King.
Tiennette, Daughter of a bondman of the Abbey of Saint Germain.
The Abbot of St Germain, Hugon de Sennecterre.
The King of France.
The Queen of France.
The King's Chamberlain.
A Fat Burgess of Paris.
A Thin One.
A Stranger.
Monks of the Abbey; a Crowd, etc., etc.,

ANSEAU DIT LE TOURANGEAU and **TIENNETTE**, meeting on a road in the Clerk's Meadow. The road has a grassy border, vines in the background and the roofs of the Abbey of Saint Germain. It is a Sunday at sunset, the Angelus ringing.

ANSEAU, a man of middle age, large, squarely built, richly dressed, black bearded, with a gold chain round his neck. Hanging from it the badge of the "Subjects of the King." He is a free man, and a burgess of the City of Paris.

TIENNETTE, a young girl, fair; dressed in sack-cloth with a rope girdle. She is leading a cow which browses in the ditch. They stand while the Angelus rings; then she passes **ANSEAU** without looking up;
ANSEAU turns and looks after her.

ANSEAU
A pretty pass,
That I, a ten years' master jeweller,
A burgess and a man of forty years
Spent soberly in service of my craft
Have not the courage for a mere "God-den "
To such a petticoat

[He calls: "Ho-la" and beckons to **TIENNETTE**. She comes back slowly, leading the cow after her.

ANSEAU
Ah, sweetheart, is your state so poor a one

That, on a Sabbath, in despite of law
You come abroad to work. Have you no fear?

TIENNETTE
My lord, I have no fear; I am below
The notice of the laws and the Lord Abbot
Doth give us licence thus to graze our cow
After the hour of vespers.

ANSEAU
Well, my dear ,
You set the welfare of your soulless beast
Above the welfare of your little soul?

TIENNETTE
Our little souls, my lord? Our soulless beast
Is more than half our lives and more than all
The little souls that we have never seen.

ANSEAU
Why, then, you're passing poor. And yet you have
Your jewels and the gold you carry with you.
Your eyes and hair; I would I had such gold.
Where are your lovers? You are near a city
Where what you have . . .

TIENNETTE
Nenny, my lord. I have . . .

[She holds out her left arm and shows him, on it, a silver band such as is worn by grazing cattle, but without the bell. **ANSEAU** raises his hands in horror.

ANSEAU
A chattel of the Abbey's . . .

TIENNETTE
Ah, my lord,
I'm daughter to the Abbey's serf Etienne.
Who marries me becomes—it makes no boot
Though he be even burgess or more great—
Becomes a bonded serf with me and falls
Body and goods to the Abbey. If he love
Withouten wedlock, then the children fall
Again to the Abbey. . . . Were I ten times less
Ill-favoured than I am, the most in love
Would flee me like the plague.

ANSEAU
And do you say
That not a one, for love of your blue eyes
And of your mouth and of your little hands.

Did ever try to buy your liberty,
As I bought mine o' the King?

TIENNETTE
It costs too dear.
It costs too dear, my lord. All those I please
At meeting go away as they did come.
It costs too dear.

ANSEAU
And have you never thought
Of seeking other lands on a good horse
Behind a rider

TIENNETTE
Oh, one thinks . . . one thinks . . .
But, sir, the Abbey's arms are very long.
They'd hang me if they caught me, and the man.
If he were noble, he must lose his lands;
If simple, life and all. I am not worth
Such stakes. Besides, I live in fear of God
Who set me where I am.

[She begins to drag the cow further along the road. **ANSEAU** stands silent. At last he says absent-mindedly:

ANSEAU
But then—your age?

TIENNETTE
I do not know, my lord, but the Lord Abbot,
They say, doth keep account

ANSEAU
And what's your name?

TIENNETTE
I have no name, my lord, my father was
Baptiz'd Etienne, and so my mother was
"The woman called Etienne," and as for me
They call me Tiennette, but I've no name.

ANSEAU [in the same tone]
Your cow, now, is a noble beast.

TIENNETTE
My lord,
Her milk's the best of all the country side.
If you do thirst. . .

ANSEAU

Why, no, I have no thirst
That that could satisfy. Now listen you
I am that Anseau called le Tourangeau,
My fame is what it is, my work no worse.
After my light I've lived and done my best,
And I am wealthy past the middle wealth.
I never followed women; ev'ry night
Your gallants passed my windows they have seen
My steadfast lamp behind the iron grilles.
Have seen me bent above the shining gold
Or black against my forge. I once was poor.
Now I am wealthy past the middle wealth.
I am a man like other men, not worse
And little better, not I think unkind
Nor too much given to mirth. And so I've lived
Since I could wield a chisel of mine own.
But now—I cannot tell you when or how,
What set me thinking, how the thought increased—
I could not sleep at night, nor brace to work.
It may have been a month; I do not know.
Till, of a sudden, as small bubbles run
To merge into one whole, the thought was there;
I must be married. I must have some soul
To share my joys with and to share my griefs,
And bear me little children Ever since
That thought has been all me. I was to-day
Before the altar of Saint Eloy's church
(The seven small gold saints and the large cross
Set with carbuncles are my proper work),
And prayed that he would set within my path
A woman fitted for my prime of life.
You see me: this is I. The air's so hot
Within the narrow streets I came out here
Where I have never walked this seven years.
The little birds were singing down the sun
The bell rang out and in the sacred minutes
I saw you stand against me; was it not
An answer from the Saint?

TIENNETTE
Alas, if but
The price were not so great.

ANSEAU
I've little skill
In women, but there is a certain sound
Comes from true metal; I've a skill in that,
And when I look at you and when you speak
I seem to hear that sound.

TIENNETTE

If but the price
Were not so great. I am not worth the tenth.
You do not know I've little skill in men.
You frighten me a little; what know I?
If there is any truth for such as I
You seem to have that truth. If any goodness
Is in the world for me, it seems in you.
You should be strong and gentle, I am weak.
I do not know; I say I do not know.
Alas, alas . . .

[She begins to weep softly. **ANSEAU** crosses himself, joins his hands and says:

ANSEAU
I make a vow to my Lord Saint Eloy, under whose invocation are all master jewellers, to invent
two shrines of gilded silver of the finest work it shall be granted to me to achieve. I make a vow to fill
them, the one with a likeness of the Holy Virgin, to the end that if I achieve the liberty of my wife,
she be glorified; the other for my patron Saint Eloy if only I have success in this my emprise. And I
swear by my eternal salvation to persevere with courage in this affair, to spend in it all that I possess
and to quit of it only with my life. So God help me, Anseau dit le Tourangeau.

[**TIENNETTE** has sunk upon her knees; **ANSEAU** bends and raises her. The cow has moved slowly up
the side of the ditch and is browsing on the vines.

TIENNETTE
Alas, alas . . .
You do not know. You must take back your vow.
I could love you all my life. Alas, alas . . .

ANSEAU
The vow is said; there is no taking back.

TIENNETTE
You do not know, alas, you do not know

[She runs to the cow as the scene closes.

SCENE II

[Paris. A place in front of the Church of St Luke. A great crowd of **BURGESSES**, their **WIVES**,
CHILDREN, **PEDLARS**, **FRIARS** and **PAGES** is round the house of Maitre Anseau.

A **STRANGER**; a **FAT BURGESS**; his **WIFE**; a **THIN BURGESS**; his **MOTHER**.

The **STRANGER**, a man in parti-coloured hose, with one long sleeve torn and hanging by a thread, a
peaked red beard, two peacock's feathers held by a brooch to a hat that has a long flap in front. He
struggles out of the **CROWD** and salutes the **FAT BURGESS**, who has his **WIFE** upon his arm.

THE STRANGER

Sir, I beseech you, sir, I am but very newly come to this town. Sir, I beseech you, tell me how I may come to the house of one

[He reads from a paper.

Maitre Anseau, dit le Tourangeau.

THE FAT BURGESS
That, sir, is the house, of stone, beside the Church. But if you would come to it you must even fly like the birds of heaven.

THE CROWD
Maitre Anseau . . . Maitre Anseau.

THE STRANGER
Sir, I am newly come to this town.
The Lord Percy is to wed, sir, and having a mind to—the Lord Percy of Northumberland—present his transcendent bride with a jewelled stomacher, and hearing of the surpassing skill of this Maitre Anseau, sent me, sir, his gentleman, sir. . . .

THE CROWD
Maitre Anseau, Maitre An . . . seau!
Cracked be all shaven skulls ... we will tear down the Abbey . . . we will . . .

THE STRANGER
And so, sir, if your master be so well be-customed, it beseems me, sir, to think that my worshipful Lord will scarce be suited, nor his transcendent bride be stomachered, this many days.

THE CROWD
Hurrah, hurrah! Be of good cheer. For the glory of Paris be skulls cracked!

THE STRANGER
I have been torn as if by wild beasts.
Behold me . . .

THE FAT BURGESS
Sir, it would seem that you know not the lamentable story. It is in this way, sir . . .

[His voice is lost in the noise of the crowd. He can he seen gesticulating. The **THIN BURGESS** interrupts him. They discuss in dumb show; the **WIVES** join the discussion. Then a lull.

THE FAT BURGESS
And so, sir, the King's Chamberlain, owing to our Master great sums for a pouncet-box set in onion stones . . .

THE THIN BURGESS
Neighbour, you mislead. I have it from Maitre Anseau himself. The pouncet-box was paid for. It was out of the great love the Chamberlain bore our master

THE FAT BURGESS
Well, be it as you will, neighbour.

For love or debt the King's Chamberlain hies him with Maitre Anseau to the Abbot. And the crafty Abbot . . .

THE CROWD
Pestilence carry off Abbot Hugon . . .
May the plague take him off ere he take one of our free burgesses for a serf.

THE FAT BURGESS
This crafty Abbot will not abate one jot; but sitteth as mum as a fox in a drain. The Master offereth great fortunes for this wench. But the Abbot will have him for a serf if he marry her, thinking to gain for the Abbey the incomparable skill of...

THE THIN BURGESS
Neighbour, you mistake. It is a matter of principle.
[To the **STRANGER**]
Sir, the thing is thus. This Abbot would enslave all us free burgesses and he makes with our Master a beginning. He hath other wenches for all us burgesses

THE WIFE OF THE THIN BURGESS
Oh, the guile, the guile. . . .

THE FAT BURGESS
Principle or no principle, the matter stands thus. Maitre Anseau going again to the Clerk's Meadow finds there no Tiennette. For, sir, our 'prentices having planned to carry her off in their despite, these wicked priests did have her clapped up close. Since which time our Master hath been suffered to see her only through a little grille. . . .

THE THIN BURGESS
See the craft of it. This is to whet his appetite.

THE FAT BURGESS'S WIFE
Oh, sir, they say it be pitiful to see them there. They do buss the bars of each side and the tears do run, do run like juice from a roasting capon. A did use to be a lusty man, and now A's grown so pale, so pale

THE FAT BURGESS
He eats not . . .

THE THIN BURGESS
Sleeps not.

THE FAT BURGESS
Does no work . . .

THE THIN BURGESS
Sighs and groans.

THE FAT BURGESS
Raves and swears . . .

THE THIN BURGESS

And the crux of the matter is: to-day he shall make his final choice, whether to have the Tiennette and a serf's life, or leave her and take to . . .

A LOUD VOICE
The King has gone to the Abbey

THE CROWD
Maitre Anseau. Mai . . .tre An . . . seau

THE THIN BURGESS
The King, sir, doth owe our
Master great sums and shall intercede for him

THE FAT BURGESS
I do wager ten yards of white velvet to a bodkin he do leave her to go her way and he his.

THE WIFE OF THE THIN BURGESS
I do wager four-score and two of my fatting capons he do have her

THE VOICE AGAIN
The King has gone to the Abbey

THE CROWD
Maitre Anseau . . . Maitre Anseau

THE FAT BURGESS
Be it a wager . . .

THE WIFE OF THE THIN BURGESS
Be it a wager and shake hands upon it

[A great uproar behind; the **CROWD** sways backwards and forwards, then opens. **MAITRE ANSEAU** is seen to be mounting a white jennet from the steps of his house.

THE CROWD
To the Abbey, to the Abbey . . .

[They run off.

THE STRANGER
I shall be killed; I shall be killed
My hat is gone.

SCENE III

[The Great Hall in the Abbey of Saint Germain. To L. very large doors, opened and showing through their arches an apple close, red apples lying in heaps on the turf below whitened tree trunks. Facing the doors the Abbot's chair. Swallows fly in and out among the gilded beams of the tall roof.

The **ABBOT HUGON, MONKS, CROSS-BEARER**. Behind—The **CROWD, SOLDIERS** of the Abbey, King's **SOLDIERS**; Afterwards—**BONDSMEN** of the Abbey.

The **ABBOT HUGON**, a very old man. His shaven face, very brown, small and dried, hangs forward on his breast, a richly jewelled mitre pressing it dawn. He is seated in his chair facing the open doors. The **MONKS** are round his chair which stands high on stone steps.

THE CROWD is being pressed in place at the back of the Hall by the **SOLDIERS** of the Abbey, who set their halberd staves across the faces. The King's **SOLDIERS** look on laughing. A great uproar. A flourish of trumpets sounds without; the **ABBOT** is assisted to his feet and gives the benediction towards the doors.

Enter the **KING** of France. He rides a black stallion into the hall; the **QUEEN** in a white litter borne by two white mules. The curtains of the litter and the clothes of the mules are sewn with golden fleur-de-lis, the mules are shod with gold. A train of **LORDS** and **LADIES** follow them. The King's **CHAMBERLAIN** comes to stand by the head of the King's horse.

THE CROWD
The King . . . the King. Do you see the King? . . . Now the Queen. Ah . . . h . . . h . . .

[The **KING** salutes the **ABBOT** who blesses him again. Their lips can be seen to move, but what they say is lost in the exclamations of the **CROWD**. . . . The **KING** bends to speak to his **CHAMBERLAIN**, who exit. The **QUEEN** puts her head out of the litter.

THE CROWD
The Queen . . . Do you see the Queen?
. . . Ah . . . h . . . h . . .

[The **CHAMBERLAIN** returns with **ANSEAU DIT LE TOURANGEAU**, "who kneels in the space between the **KING** and the **ABBOT**.

THE CROWD [a great cry]
Ha, Maitre Anseau,
Maitre Anseau. A free man. No serf. . . no serf. . . .

[It grows silent. The voice of the **KING** is heard as if continuing a speech.

KING
Be of good courage, man.
My lord the Abbot will have need of us
Upon a day.

THE CROWD
Huzza . . . hear the King . . . the King

KING
For in the end, we are the King of
France.
If what men say be true we are more poor
Than you are. Therefore courage, man, look up.
Set a high price and with a smiling face

Cast down that price. Lord Abbot name it him.
He's stores of gold, they say. Now, Master, rise.
Stand up, man, and unpouch. Lord Abbot, name
The lowest ransom.

ABBOT
Sire, the price is fixt.

THE CROWD
Strangle that Abbot. Cast him down to us.

ABBOT
The price is fixt. There is one only price.
I am the servant of the Abbey's fame.
Glory, renown and ancient heritages.
Our statutes fix the price, I can no more.
We live in troublous times; the breakers roar
Against the ship o' the Church; the times are evil;
And I a feeble, poor old man who stand
By the grace of God at the helm. What would you have?
To bate one jot of our enforced rights
Were to cast down into that raging sea
One of the sails we trust to for our voyage
And final harbouring. The price is fixt.

THE CROWD
Let us unfix it. Cast him down to us.

KING
You hear him, Master?

ANSEAU
Oh, I hear him, sire.

KING [To his **CHAMBERLAIN**]
You should be famous to defeat the laws,
To find out quibbles; cheat the statutes' due.
What say you?

CHAMBERLAIN
Sire, I can but what I can.
The Abbot is too strong; 'tis manifest
That he who's certain of the whole would be
Ill skilled at bargaining to take a part.
The Abbot's case is that. And for the rest:
I've argued with our Master; I have said:
"Good Master, think, the world is very large.
And full t'o'erflowing of dames passing fair."
I've told him that the tenth part of his goods
Would purchase him the name of nobleman.
Another tenth a lady to his bed.

The noblest and the fairest in the land.
What would you have? The man is made of iron
And will not bend; the Abbot will not break.
And I have wasted breath.

KING
Good madam Queen,
Entreat my lord the Abbot for these lovers.

QUEEN
My lord, I've done a many things for you.
Have broidered copes, have made my ladies sew.
Your altar cloths with pearls. Beseech you now
Have pity on these lovers.

ABBOT
Oh, fair Queen,
In that I am a man I pity them.
In that I am God's servant I must shut
My eyes, my ears, my heart. Since there have been
An abbey in this place, and monks and bondsmen—
As who should say: Through all the mists of time.
It hath not been decreed that there should fall
A burgess of the city to the Abbey.
If now this precedent should be despised
There would not . . .

QUEEN
Oh, a truce to precedent.
What is this wench? A girl who leads a cow;
In sackcloth. Doth the honour of the Abbey
Depend on girls in sackcloth?

ABBOT
Oh, fair Queen,
The precedent . . .

QUEEN
Depends on girls in sackcloth!
Good, my lord Abbot, I had thought you wise,
Old learned Churchmen had had better wits.
What you? a man of three-and-ninety years
Who by the very nature of your vows
Are closured out from love ... to say a wench
That leads a cow is necessary to
The honour of your Abbey

ABBOT
Lady Queen,
I am an old man; doting I do say:
This wench that leads a cow is necessary

To the honour of our Abbey

KING
Gentle wife.
You have the Abbot on the hip, but sweet,
A-meanwhiles our good Master kneels on thorns.
Lord Abbot, make an end; produce this wench,
This Helen that doth rive our world in twain,
And let our Master make his utter choice.

[At a sign from **ABBOT HUGON**, four-and-twenty **ACOLYTES** issue out from behind the chair. They strew white rose petals upon the steps until it is like a hill of snow. Enter **TIENNETTE**.

THE CROWD
Ah . . . h . . . h . . .

[**TIENNETTE** is dressed like a maiden-queen in white, with a white coif sewn with gold, with a girdle of silver filigree, with white gloves embroidered with pearls. The **ABBOT HUGON** beckons to her to mount the steps to him. She does so.

KING [to **MAITRE ANSEAU**]
Nay, man, hadst well be wealthier than we
To set a price on her that led your cow.
[To the **ABBOT**]
If you will do us favour in this thing.
We shall requite you. We are France and Paris. . . .

THE CROWD
Paris and France! . . .

KING
And France and Paris have been touched home
By fortunes of these lovers Hear us roar! . . .

THE CROWD
Paris and France!

ABBOT
Ah, sire, what would you do?
You touch yourself by melling in this thing.
If we should blench to this unquiet mob
They would gain strength from broken precedent
Which is a dyke against this hungry sea
Wherein a breach being made, the sea sweeps in
And overwhelms us . . . overwhelms all France,
The Abbey and the Court

THE CROWD
Paris and France.

KING [to them]

Nenny, ye lend the Abbot similes
That are not pleasant savoured. Master speak

[**MAITRE ANSEAU** has risen to his feet and advances towards the **ABBOT** holding out his arms.

QUEEN [to her **LADIES**]
She's fair; why, yes,
I think she's fair to see.
She halts a little. But she's fair, she's fair.

ANSEAU
Oh, Father Abbot, oh, you man of God,
If you have any pity in your heart,
If you have any hope of rest to come,
Bethink you, oh, bethink you. It grows late,
You stand upon the very verge of the shade
Death casts upon us. I do know the law
And I have made a vow. But, man of God,
The thing is in your hands. For me remains
No choice. The verdict lies with you. For me . . .
I have been poor, and I have been a bondsman.
And I am patient, oh! and I can bear.
But oh, you man of God, take heed, take heed.
If you have ever seen a little child,
And if your frozen eyes have thawed to see
The sunlight on the little children's faces.
Bethink you of the curse you cast upon
The children that that maid shall bear to me.
I have no choice, I have made the vow to God
And I fulfil it. But the little children . . .
Have you the heart to let them live that life,
Un-named, unknown, to live and die as beasts
That perish; all those tender little things
That God doth mean should burgeon in the light
And with their little laughter sing his praise.

ABBOT
I am a very ancient man, and stand
Within the shadow, and I stand and say:
The price is fixt.

ANSEAU
Accursed rat o' the Church,
The price is fixt ... is fixt. Oh, horrible.
Insensate thirst for gold. Then, oh, thou man.
Thou spider gorging on the brink of hell.
Suck up my gold, my life. But oh, I keep
The better part of me, you cannot touch
The subtle engine God hath pleased to fix
Within my brain, you cannot use the skill
That made me what I am. And that I swear

Not torture, not the rack, not death itself
Shall set in motion. All your Abbey's rents
For twice a hundred years could never pay
What it shall lose thereby. I am more strong
Than iron's hard, and the more long-suffering
Than grief is great. For you I might have been
A fashioner of things divine; for you
I shall be but a pack-horse.

[**TIENNETTE**, who had covered her face with her arms, stretches out her arms to **ANSEAU**.

TIENNETTE
Oh, my love,
My lord, my more than life, thou noble man.
Forsake me, oh, forsake me, I did say
"You did not know," and, oh you did not know.
When you did make your vow. Forsake me, then,
And go your ways

ANSEAU
I cannot go my way;
I have no way but only this with you.

TIENNETTE
There is a way that God hath shown to me—
These last few weeks they have been schooling me
Within their cloisters—and there is a way,
By which, if you do love me more than all,
You shall enjoy me and go free in the end.
For this the law is—they have told me so—
If I should die before a child is born.
You should go free though losing house and store.
The occasion of your serfdom being dead.
And oh, my lord and life.
You shall. But for my sin of laying hands
Upon myself, full surely the Lord God
Shall pardon me, full surely the Lord God
Shall pardon who doth know and weigh all hearts.

[**THE ABBOT** lays his hand upon her arm.

THE CROWD
You shall not hurt her; we will have you down.
Old Spider . . . Rat o' the Church.

KING
Ah, make an end,
Lord Abbot, for our dames have eyes all wet.

ABBOT
The price is fixt.

ANSEAU
And I must pay the price.

THE CROWD
You shall not; no, you shall not. We are the free burgesses of Paris.

[The **ABBOT HUGON** beckons Maitre **ABBOT ANSEAU** to come tip to him. He slowly ascends the steps. The thurifers draw round and a cloud of incense goes up. The **MONKS** chant and the **KING** removes his heaver. The **QUEEN** and her **LADIES** cross themselves.

A great uproar in the hall; the **SOLDIERS** of the Abbey are thrown down and the **CROWD** breaks through; the King's **SOLDIERS** force it back. The sound of hells comes in from, without. Enter the **BONDSMEN** of the Abbey bearing a canopy. The **ABBOT** is seen blessing **ANSEAU** and **TIENNETTE**. Afterwards they go down the steps together. A **MONK** beckons them to stand beneath the canopy, which has gold staves with little silver bells. During this wedding there has been a constant clamour. Now it falls silent.

ABBOT
Anseau, thou serf and bondsman of our Abbey,
Acknowledge that thy goods and life are ours.

ANSEAU
I do acknowledge it.

THE ABBOT [to the **BONDSMEN**]
Bare ye his arm.
Up to the elbow. Armourer, set thou on
This bondsman's wrist the shackle of his state.

[The **ARMOURER** rivets a silver collar upon the arm of **ANSEAU**. Whilst he is doing it the **ABBOT** descends the steps and comes to them.

ABBOT
My hands are very feeble, I am old.
[To **TIENNETTE**]
Give me some help, thou wife of the new bondsman.

[The **ABBOT HUGON** undoes the collar from the arm of **ANSEAU**.

THE CROWD
Ah . . . h . . . h . . . What is this? What is this?

ABBOT [To **MAITRE ANSEAU**]
Thou art a master jeweller. Hast skill
To break the collar from thy new wife's arm
And not to hurt her?

[**ANSEAU** stands as if amazed. The **ABBOT** frees **TIENNETTE**.

Lo, thou burgess's wife,

How is it, to be free?

THE CROWD
What? . . . what . . . What is this? . . . Are they free?

[As the curtain falls **ANSEAU** and **TIENNETTE** stand as if amazed. The **MONKS** raise their hands in horror.

THE AFTER SCENE

[The Chamber of the **ABBOT**. A hare, small, white-washed room. On the floor, in a broad ray of sunlight that falls from the barred windows, stand two great gilt shrines. The door of the one is closed; through the half-opened doors of the other one sees an image of the Virgin in the likeness of **TIENNETTE** having a little **CHILD** upon her arm and a cow kneeling at her feet.

ABBOTT
Two Religious.

[The **ABBOT** lies with his eyes closed upon a narrow pallet, a black rosary falling from his clasped hands.

[The **TWO RELIGIOUS** stand motionless, their heads covered by their cowls, at his feet.

[A long silence in which is heard the cooing of a blue pigeon on the window-sill. The **ABBOT** opens his eyes.

ABBOT
So ye are there; I sent for you. The end Is very near me now.

[He makes a weak gesture with one hand as if pointing to the shrines.

You see those things?
What say you, brothers, did I dote? I know,
I say I know, have known this many months
What you have whispered in the refectory.
"The Abbot dotes," you said, "The Abbot dotes" . . .
You said I doted; that my heart was touched
By whimperings of lovers. One of you
Shall step into my shoes a short day hence.
Oh, let your dotage work as well as mine
For honour of the Abbey; do but once
One-half of what I did in this one thing!
You said I doted, that my heart was touched.
Nenny, I have a heart, but I am old
And very cunning. I have seen more things
Than most. And I do know my world, I say.
You would have kept him, you. My heart was touched,
In happy hour, I say, my heart was touched.
Mine that has nursed the Abbey's honour here

As mothers nurse their babes. You would have held
The letter of the law and raised a storm.
That had cast down our house. . . . The burgesses
Do love us now; this twelvemonth they have brought
More offerings than in a lustre past.
You would have kept the law and raised a storm
That must have shorn us of one-half the rights
We have upon the city. I did know
That, in the acclamations of my mercy
The collar I have set upon their necks
Would gall no withers, yet the precedent
Be riveted. And there is more than this
I gained whose heart was touched by lovers' tears.
It brought us these two shrines. I tell you, men,
I prophesy who lie at the point of death.
That when all precedents are swept away,
And you and I and all of us become
A little dust that would not fill a cup,
These shrines shall be the glory of the Abbey,
Its chiefest profit and most high renown.
For men shall marvel at the handiwork,
And women tell the story at their work,
And crossed lovers come from all the lands
To make their offerings and shed salt tears
Unto the saints that let their hearts be moved
By these two lovers of the time before.
I prophesy.
Upon the point of death, I know my world,
I have been in it for a mort of years. . . .
And one of you shall step into my shoes.
You stand there thinking it; I know my world.

[He closes his eyes, then opens them and looks at the image of the Virgin.

Oh, blessed child upon thy mother's arm,
Remember when our Brotherhood is tried
[To the **RELIGIOUS**]
Go, get ye to your whisperings again
And say I doted
Brothers, go with God.
Send me a little wine and let me sleep.

[He closes his eyes again. Exeunt the **RELIGIOUS**. The blue pigeon flies from the window-sill. Its wings
clatter in the stillness.

KING COPHETUA'S WOOING

A SONG DRAMA IN ONE ACT

Dramatis Personae
Cophetua, King.
Christine, A Beggar Maid.

[Scene discovers **COPHETUA**, dressed as a beggar, seated beneath a thorn on a hillside. In the distance, a road running down to the sea; at the verge a small chapel.

An early morning in May.

COPHETUA
Could I but keep my beggar's staff,
And change my cares for my beggar's laugh,
And keep my gown with its sleeve and a half,
And just lay down my orb and crown,
I think my heart would weigh more light.
And I should sleep more sound at night.
But the day's come round, and sweet Christine
Must doff her robe of faded green
And know herself for a burdened Queen.

[To him enters the **CHRISTINE**, the Beggar Maid.

CHRISTINE
Here am I in my bridal attire;
I sat all night by the fire
And stitched in the sheltered byre,
And the sun is so bright
And my heart is so light
It hasn't a care, and it's all your own.
It's yours, just yours, and yours alone.

COPHETUA
Last night I dreamt a weary thing,
That you were you and I the King,
With a heart so sad I could not sing.
And I came pricking along the way
And you sat here beneath the may.

CHRISTINE
Lay off your dreams, the church bell rings,
And were you ten times king of kings.
And ten times Kaiser, you could be
No more a king than you're king of me.

COPHETUA
If I were King and made you Queen?

CHRISTINE
And were I that, would the green-wood sheen
Be a whit less glad or the gay green sward

Less dear were you King and Over-lord?
Would you love me less? I trow not so.

I saw the King a while ago
Go pricking by with his haughty crew
While I sat here in the morning dew
Before I ever thought of you.

He cast me this rose noble. See!
And I thought, "This shall be my wedding fee
To the man I love and the man I wed."
(I've thought when I looked at the good King's head
That the noble bears, that he favours you
In the nose and the mouth and the forehead too.)

COPHETUA
But if I made you Queen . . .

CHRISTINE
What yet
I' the track o' dreams, see! I will set
My hawthorn crown upon your brow;
The dew hangs on it even now.
And where is there a fairer gem
Set in a fair queen's diadem
Than this one lustrous drop?

COPHETUA
Christine,
What if I made you such a Queen?
There is a cloud doth dimn my mind
But if....

CHRISTINE
Oh, love . . .

[The bell sounds down the wind.

The priest will soon pass down the hill.
And we're to wed, and you are dreaming still.

COPHETUA [speaking after a long pause]
I love your face, I love your hands, your eyes
Are pools of rest for mine. I love your feet,
Your little shoes, the patches in your gown . . .

CHRISTINE
I know your tongue now . . .

COPHETUA.
If I make you Queen . . .

CHRISTINE
I would all "ifs" were sunk beneath the sea—
There is a proverb ties them to us beggars—
And make, why make, not made?

COPHETUA
It was a thought,
A passing cloud—the shadow of a dream.

CHRISTINE
Ah, love, no more of dreams, they frighten me.
The sun is up, look at the streak of sea
Between the hills. And love—no more of dreams.
The larks thrill all above the downs with songs
To shatter dreams. And there's a song about it:
[singing]
"If you and I were King and Queen,"
I'll sing it if you'll join me in the lilt;
I'd rather sing than dream the time away.
[she sings]
If you and I were King and Queen
[a silence]
Now join me if you love me, dream if not.
[she sings again]
She. If you and I were King and Queen—

He. Sweet Christine—

She. Would you come courting me?

He. You should see.

She. Would a crown spoil my face,
Or a throne mar my grace?
Would you keep me the same high place in your heart?
Must we still part to meet, should we still meet to part,
If we were King and Queen?

Together. Ah then! ah then!
How should we fare with our cates rich and rare,
We beggars, we lovers of roadsides, we rovers
Of woodlands and townlands and dalelands and downlands?
We lovers . . .

[**COPHETUA** is silent and the song ceases.

CHRISTINE
I think you do not love me any more,
Now you forget my songs.

COPHETUA

I cannot think of songs, nor hear the lark,
Nor feel the glad spring weather. In my ears
Is nothing but the tramping of the hoofs,
And in my eyes the flash of swords and silks
Of a proud cavalcade that comes anow
To bear us hence.

CHRISTINE

Oh, God, your mind is sprung,
Your thoughts, gone wand'ring into other fields,
Have left poor me in mine.

COPHETUA

Not so, not so;
My mind's come back from long sweet sojournings
In a free land of hill and down and sea.
To a sad world of walled towns and courts
And carks and cares.

CHRISTINE

No, no, the sun's there yet.

COPHETUA

He shines no more on me—no more on me,
I am a King again—a King—and you
Must either leave the life you love, to lead
With me the life I loathe, or let me live
Alone, unaided, all alone and sad,
The life that leads a King.

CHRISTINE

There is a weary horror in your eyes.
And I must needs believe you. I'm a beggar,
So were my sire before me and his sires,
For generations and for ages past
We've lived free lives and breathed the good free air
You came among us in a free man's guise
And wooed me—wooed me—and I gave my heart
To you a freeman.

COPHETUA

Oh—a weary King . . .
For a short breathing space I doffed my crown.
Laid down my cares and walked without a load.
The task remains myself did set myself
Duly to reign, to shape a people's ends.
As I deem just. Here have I neither end
Of travel, nor an aim for life to hit,
Or miss i' the shooting.

CHRISTINE
Could we not live free?

COPHETUA
Not free, not free, my task would call me back.
It calls me now. It calls me, calls me now.

CHRISTINE
Is this all true, no summer morning's dream?
Oh, here is then that parting of the ways
I dreamt of yesternight.

COPHETUA
There lie the roads,
Here travel I.

CHRISTINE
And I must choose, must choose
Between my love and life, the old free life.
Then choose I this, in good or evil weather.
Up hill or down, on moorland and in fen.
On white sea sand or 'mid the purple heather.
To travel on with you, and where or when
The mists o'erwhelm us, meet them, and together
Uphold with you the burden and the pain.
Oh, all the love I bore you and still bear you
Make light our feet, and temper time and tide.
And each day's setting out shall find me near you,
And each day's close shall find me at your side.

[A long pause. At last.

CHRISTINE
And it was you rode by upon the horse?

COPHETUA
And you it was sat there upon a stone—
But hark, ah hark, there wind the distant horns.
They come, they come, the old free life is passing.

CHRISTINE
Oh, hide me from their eyes, such cruel eyes
They had that rode with you that day of days.

COPHETUA
Those are the eyes must look upon us now
For ever and for ever till the end.

CHRISTINE
The horns, the horns, the old free life is passing.

COPHETUA
Oh, yonder, there's the glimpse of sun on steel,
And there's my oriflamme. And there,
Beyond the chapel, is another band
Comes trooping from the ships.

CHRISTINE
They come, they come,
The old free life is passing.

COPHETUA
It is past,
The bell has ceased to toll.

CHRISTINE
Oh, let us wait,
I could not bear their eyes. Oh, clasp me round.
And let me die to-day.

COPHETUA
You must be bold,
And there, before the altar, shame them all.

CHRISTINE
Ah, there, before the altar, I'll be proud.
And show them all a brow serene and clear
For love of you. But now I'm what I am.
And needs must tremble for the time to come.

COPHETUA.
The horns have played their last and we must go.

CHRISTINE
You know the old lament they sing at sea
When the last rope's cast off. My dear dead father
Would have us sing it just before he died.
We'll never sing again, for brooding hearts
Cry, "Silent, voices, hush," and now we sail,
And sing to drown our thoughts and singing, die.
So now set sail, set sail. Loose the last rope
That binds us to the past.

[As they go, she sings "The Farewell of those that go away in ships."

[**CHRISTINE** sings.

Fare thee well, land o' home
(Oh, the sea, the sea's a foam)
Fare thee well, land o' home.
        Blue and low.
Fare thee well, house o' home, where the mellow wall-fruits grow,

Old fields, fields o' home, where the yellow paigles glow.
Fare thee well, land o' home.
        Blue and low.
Fare thee well, pleasant land
(Ah the foam beats on the strand)
Fare thee well, my forbear's land
        Blue and low.
Fare thee well, mother mine, with the pure pale brow,
Fare ye well, quiet graves, fare ye well who rest below.
Fare thee well, land o' home.
Over miles and miles of foam,
Fare thee well, land o' home.
        Blue and low.

"THE MOTHER"

A SONG DRAMA

Dramatis Personae
The Spirit of the Age
The Mother
The Little Blades of Grass
The Little Grains of Sand and of Dust

Scene.—Just outside a great city. Battalions of staring, dun-coloured, brick houses, newly finished, with "vacant windows, bluish slate roofs and yellow chimney pots, march on the fields which are blackened and shrouded with fog. Innumerahle lInes of railway disappear among them, gleaming in parallel curves. Fog signals sound and three trains pass on different levels; the lights in their windows an orange blur. A continuous hooting of railway engines. **THE SPIRIT OF THE AGE**, leaning on the brick parapet of the upper embankment, speaks towards The **MOTHER**, who is unseen in the fog above the fields.

THE SPIRIT OF THE AGE
It's I have conquered you.
It is over and done with your green and over and done with your blue.
Conquered you. Where is your sky?
Where is the green that your gown had of late?

THE MOTHER
Wait.

THE SPIRIT OF THE AGE
I have trampled you down, you must die.
It is only begun
Yet it's over and done
With the green of your grass and the blue of your sky.
Even your great constellations
Blaze vainly, are hid by the dun
Of the smoke of my fires

THE MOTHER
I wait; I have patience.

THE SPIRIT OF THE AGE
The smoke of my fires,
The dun of the lives and desires
Of the millions and millions who live
And who strive.
Only to trample you down, blot you out, foul your face and forget.

THE MOTHER
Ah, and yet.

[The fog to the north lifts a little and discloses clouds of smoke like a pall above a forest of chimney stacks; a square Board School playground where **CHILDREN** are running through puddles on the wet asphalt.

THE SPIRIT OF THE AGE
And behold, they are toiling and moiling
And soiling
Your winds and your rains; yea, and hark to the noise
Of the girls and the boys
Of untold generations.

THE MOTHER
I wait. I have patience.

THE SPIRIT OF THE AGE
They play in the waters
I grant them, the daughters
Of fog-dripped smut-showers.
Would they thank you for flowers
Or know how to play by your Ocean's blown billows?
Who never met you.
Whose sires forget you.
These nations and nations
Who never saw sea nor the riverside willows.

THE MOTHER
I wait; I have patience.

THE SPIRIT OF THE AGE
Old Silence, wait; old Sleeper, use your patience.
You are dead and forgotten
As a corpse that was rotten
A twelvemonth and more;
As dead as the Empires of yore.
As dead and forgotten.

THE LITTLE GRAINS OF SAND [Whispering]

Listen, listen.

THE LITTLE GRAINS OF SAND [Whispering]
Ah, we hear; you'll see us glisten
When the Wind shall set us whirling.

THE SPIRIT OF THE AGE
I am here and I shall stay
To the utter, utter day;
Tell me, you who've lived for ever,
Saw you ever such a fever,
Such a madness of gold-getting.
Such forgetting
Of the Thing that you called Truth—
Such contempt, such lack of ruth,
For your leisure and your dalliance,
As since Time and I joined alliance?
I shall rule and falter never.
You are dead and gone for ever.

[He pauses. **THE MOTHER** says nothing.

THE LITTLE BLADES OF GRASS [Whispering]
Are you there, O all ye others?

THE LITTLE GRAINS OF SAND
We are here, O little brothers.

THE SPIRIT OF THE AGE
 Old Silence, speak!
I had not thought to find you half so weak
In argument. Acknowledge I am he
That ever more shall be.
Be just; confess that I have won
And that your race is run.

[She still keeps silence. He goes on, excitedly.

D'you think that I am frightened by your fools
Who with their rules
And rusty saws from musty stools
In dusty schools.
Squeak. "In the very nature of the case,
Unless the sequence of the immobile earth
Shall change, the sun and tides stand still and all
The vast phenomena of peoples, kings.
And mighty Empires be for you reversed.
That day must come when your world-sway declines"?

THE LITTLE BLADES OF GRASS
Hearken, hearken:

Brothers, are ye there?

THE LITTLE GRAINS OF SAND
Brothers, when that wind blows we shall darken
All the air.

THE SPIRIT OF THE AGE
 I heard another fool with: "Time shall come
When the tired human brain,
That now already reels,
Shall utterly refuse to face again
The turmoil and the hum
Of all these wheels and wheels and wheels and wheels and wheels,
This clattering of feet
And hurrying no-whither; deem it sweet
To lie among the grasses,
Where no more shadow is than of the cloud that passes
Beneath the sun." Another squeaked of strife;
Of cataclysms, plagues; and slackening grip on life,
And pictured for us street on street on street
Re-echoing to the feet
Of one sole, panic-stricken passenger;
Pictured ray houses roofless to the air.
The windows glassless, doors with ruined locks,
The owlet and the fox
Sole harbourers there;
The only sounds hawks' screaming, plover's shriek
Above the misted swamps; the rivers burst
Their banks and sweep, athirst,
My rotting city Horrid! . . . Mother, speak;
Speak, mother, speak, who are so old and wise.

THE LITTLE BLADES OF GRASS [Tittering]
Ho, ho! ho, ho!
The braggart groweth tremulous.

THE LITTLE GRAINS OF SAND AND OF DUST
Hallo! hallo—o—o!
He is afraid of us.

THE SPIRIT OF THE AGE
 D'you think that I am frighted by these lies?
Old Dotard, I . . .
I rule; am come to stay
For ever and a day.
Behold,
Where all my million lieges toil for grime and gold.

[The fog lifts suddenly. Against a shaft of pale, golden sky, one sees the immense City like a watery-
edged silhouette. A great central dome, the outlines wet and gilded by the rays of light; warehouses

like black iron cliffs, square along a river; black barges, with pale lights at the bows, creeping down the glassy yellow water; forests of chimney stacks and of masts of shipping.

Answer, old witch; old silent envier of my joy,
I challenge you, old Hecate.

THE MOTHER [Very softly]
Where is Troy?

THE SPIRIT OF THE AGE
 What's Troy compared to me?

THE MOTHER
 Where Carthage, Nineve,
Where Greece, where Egypt, where are all that host
Whose very names are lost?

THE LITTLE BLADES OF GRASS [Whispering]
When we crave them.
Then we have them.

THE LITTLE GRAINS OF SAND AND OF DUST
When the winds blow we o'er-ride them.
And we hide them
Silently.

THE SPIRIT OF THE AGE
 What were they all—all of them measured by me?
For never among the Nations
And never between the Oceans,
Were known such emanations
Of tense, strung-nerved emotions,
Such strivings,
Never such hivings
Of humans.

THE MOTHER
 Son, those cities of the plain and of the shore!
My winds blew and their fleets were shattered,
My waves raged their harbours a-choke;
A very little their strivings mattered,
Little their tenseness; their hivings broke
For evermore.
Little one, I who am young, furnished them graves and I sung
Dirges above them. You have your millions.
Men of all nations, I have my billions and billions and billions.
Of those who are stronger than men; whose persistence.
Whose creeping on sods, and flight down the winds
evades the last watch, overpowers the hopeless resistance.

THE LITTLE BLADES OF GRASS

Hearken, hearken:
Brothers, are ye there?

THE LITTLE GRAINS OF SAND AND OF DUST
Brothers, when that wind blows we shall darken
All the air.

THE MOTHER
 Son: when I turn in my slumber,
Your cities withouten number
Shall fall There shall remain upon the ground
Rubble and rubbish; a rising and settling of dust all round.
Here and there a mound
And the grass will come a-creeping.
And the sands come sifting, sweeping,
Down the winds and up the current.
Dry and dead and curst, abhorrent.
Grass for the cities of the plains and of the hills; sand and bitter dust for the cities of the shore.
Little one, I who am old, hid all those strivings of yore,
Little one, i old and grey.
Bid you play.
Wrestle and worry and play in the folds of my dress.
Till you tire, and the fire of your passions fails in your earth-weariness.
Little one, I who am kind, give you time till you tire of your play.
Time till you weary and say:
"Hold; enough of our making-believe.
Ah, children, leave striving and leave
The little small things that we deemed
Above price; all the playthings that seemed
Worth a world of contriving and strife."
When the glimmer of gold loses life
And its weight groweth deader and deader.
And no one shall crave to be leader,
O'ermasterer, lord of the knife.
Little one, I who am wise, bid you go back to your play.
Play the swift game thro' the day.
When even comes you shall kneel down and pray.
And, well-content, at last lay down your head
Upon my ultimate bed
And lose the tenseness of your futile quest
In me who offer rest.

[The fog sweeps down: the city disappears. **THE SPIRIT OF THE AGE** says in a low voice.

Poor wand'ring proser,
Poor worn-out, mutt'ring dozer,
With your old saws
Of sempiternal laws,
The day's to me not you . . .
Strike down the old; cry onwards to the new.

[A train rumbles slowly past, going cautiously through the yellow fog.

THE LITTLE BLADES OF GRASS [Whispering]
Hearken, hearken:
Brothers, are ye there?

THE LITTLE GRAINS OF SAND AND DUST [Whispering back]
Brothers, when that wind blows we shall darken
All the air.

Curtain.

THE FACE OF THE NIGHT

A PASTORAL

*The men of Gnossos have a legend that a man lying all night in the marshes near that town may see
a face looking down upon him out of the sky. Such a man shall ever after be consumed with a longing
to see again that face. In pursuit of it he shall abandon his home, his flocks and his duty to the State.
And such men are accounted blasphemers because they infect others with this fever and are harmful
to the republic.*

[A wide, stony plain, the bed of a river, but dry and brown because it is the heart of summer.
Towards sunset. In the distance against the sky there rise the columns of a deserted temple and of
poplar trees with, at their bases, a tangle of rosebushes and of underwood among fallen stones. To
the right, far off, is a rocky bluff, purple against the evening: at its foot, very clear and small, are
large fallen rocks round a green pool and spreading and shadowy trees. Small fires glimmer here. To
the left the plain opens out towards the horizon, wide, suave and level; at the verge is a shimmer of
the broad curve of the river.

In the foreground a **YOUNG MAN** lies upon two fleeces. A fillet has fallen from his hair, his limbs are
a golden brown, he has a leopard skin about his loins. His hands are clasped behind his head, he
looks up into the western sky, his eye searching for the first planet to shine. Over the plain from the
sunset and from the sheepfolds in the shadow of the bluff, **YOUNG GIRLS** and **SHEPHERDS** come
towards him in knots. Some play upon pipes, others cry out from band to band, a horn sounds faintly
with a guttural intonation. A dog's bark winds sharply from a distance, and there is a continual drone
of gnats in the still air.

THE YOUNG MAN [Listlessly]
I have seen the Night with her hair gemm'd with stars,
With her smile the Milky Way, and her locks the darker bars
Of the heavens. . . .

THE SHEPHERDS AND THE YOUNG GIRLS
Oh, come away,
For Lalage is thine.
I have seen her.

HE

With her pale face of stars

THEY
Rise! The shine
Of the owl-light's on the pools,
And the hinds bring skins of wine,
And the hot day cools
To its close.

[The drone of the pipes and the quivering of strings still sound as others come across the plain. They come closer, and, standing round, obscure the sky from him.

HE [Rising on one elbow]
Ah! still your pipes, still the cyther string that jars.
For I have seen the Night with her face of stars.

THE MEN
Rise up and quit these places, for in shadows Lalage
Awaits thee.

THE GIRLS.
Quit your fleeces, for in the shadows we
In the light of nuptial torches where the poplars bar the sky.
Thro' the rocks around the pool, thro' the hyacinths shall . . .

HE
I,
I have seen, have seen. . . .

AN OLD MAN [Hastening upon them]
Why never,
Quit these places full of fever.

HE
I saw a face look downwards
Thro' the stars.

OLD MAN
No, never, never.

HE
I did see . . .

OLD MAN [seeking to drown his voice]
Mists from the river.

A YOUNG GIRL'S VOICE [She sings as she comes along]
When he comes from seawards,
When he comes from townwards.
My love sings to me words
That my heart likes well.

THE MEN [To him]
We will bear thee on our shoulders
Through the covert-sides and boulders
With thy fleeces for a litter.

THE GIRLS
Unto where the watch-fires glitter
On our shoulders we will bear thee
To where Lalagé shall rear thee
'Twixt her breasts.

HE
A face looked downwards,
And I thirst, I thirst, am thirsting.

OLD MAN [In a threatening whisper]
Close thy lips on this for ever.
This is blasphemy. 'Twould sever
Life and love and earth from gladness.
Close thy lips. I know this madness.
I am ancient.

HE
I am thirsting.

A YOUNG MAN
Thy Lalagé's eyes are pools of rest,
Thy Lalagé's lips are sweet warm grapes
I would it were mine to taste and taste.

A YOUNG GIRL
And thy Lalagé's heart is bursting.

THE YOUNG MAN
I would it were mine to sink and sink
Between her breasts like hills of wine.
I would it were mine
To taste her lips,
And to clasp her hips and to clasp her waist,
And to drink her breath and to be the first
To...

HE
Thirst. I thirst.

TWO GIRLS [With horns slung from their shoulders]
Here is milk. Here wine.

HE
Begone and send me that wind to drink

That cools its flood on the glacier's brink,
Send me that wind.

OLD MAN [persuasively]
Thy Lalagé is grown kind:
Sighs fill the air near her, and from her eyes,
Where low she lies upon the filmy fleeces,
Bright tears down fall into the milk-white creases.
And warm, dark valleys of her snowy kirtle.
And loosely tied her girdle. . . .

A HERO [Running in on them]
Thy white ewe hath burst her hurdle.
Thy grey bitch hath tree'd a leopard,
Shepherd, shepherd.
Thy black heifer's milk doth curdle.

HE [With a weary and passionate gesture of disgust]
I am sick of sheep and shepherds.

THE MEN
Thou hast led us in the wars!

THE GIRLS
And the fairest of us maidens opens out to you her arms.
Round her feet the grasses whisper, round her head the firefly swarms
Form a beacon, you shall harbour in her soft, warm arms.

HE
I did see a face with for hair the darker bars
Of the heavens. . . .

THE GIRLS [Seeking to drown his voice]
We'll go dancing where the torchlights meet
With the lances of the starlight and the grove is shadowiest,
Showing here a foam-white shoulder, white-waved arm and red lit breast.
As the harebells brush our ankles till our loves caress our feet,
Burnt-out torches, rustling silence, and the night wind's faint and fleet.

HE [Turning upon his elbow towards the **MEN**]
I shall lead you with your lances when you face the Men of Hather?
I must voice you in the counsels of the aged king, my father?
I shall lead the ships to seawards, I must guard the flocks from townwards?
[To the **GIRLS**]
I must bed your fairest maidens that the rest may dance in cadence?
So that wine may flow in plenty, so your loves and you content ye.
Whilst with chitons loose on shoulders in the twilight of the boulders.
And in secret dells
Ye wantons! I have seen a face look downwards,
Pure and passionless and distant where with stars the pure sky teemeth.

OLD MAN
He blasphemeth, he blasphemeth.

HE
I am sick of vine-wreathed barrels,
Sick of lances, arrows, quarrels,
Sick of tracking in the dew.
Of their limbs, and breasts, and you
I have seen that face effaces,
I have thought the utter thought.

[**HE** rises to his feet.

I go to seek in desert places.

[Whilst he speaks the **MEN** heave up stones to throw at him. The **GIRLS** shake their hands and cry out. He silences them, shaking his fist. The **OLD MAN** runs about behind whispering to one and another.

HE
[To the **GIRLS**]
All your sun-tanned arms are nought.
All their lances and your dances.
Nought and nought And I must wander
Past the mountains of Iskander,
Past the salt-glazed lakes of Meine,
Past Pahan mist-veiled and rainy.
Whither? Whither? Ah, my Fortune?
Seeking her, I must importune
All the icy ghosts of souls
That died of frost, and all the ghouls
That feed in battle-clouds.
The fiery spirits in the shrouds
Above volcanoes and the spirits of the dawn
That sing in choirs. And where the caverns yawn
Which let out sleep, and death, and shame, and leprosy
Upon this earth, you may find trace of me
But here no more.

OLD MAN
Blasphemy! Blasphemy!
He doth contemn this godlike life of ours.

THE GIRLS
Blasphemy! Blasphemy!
He doth condemn our warm, sweet midnight hours.

HE [Moving away from the plain]
I must go seek her on the icy rocks,
Frost in my blood or flame about my head,
Calling and calling where the echo mocks,

Crying in the midnights where the ocean moans
White in the darkness

[A **MAN** casts a great stone that strikes him on the shoulder. He falls on to one knee.

Fool, though I be dead
All here is nothing, but in her fair places
My shade shall find her wisdom.

THE GIRLS
Stones! Cast stones!

[A shower of stones strikes him down. He cries from the ground.

All here is nothing. Whilst each mountain traces
Shadows half-circling from every worthless dawn.
My shade shall trace her to her twilit portal.
Then, on a hill-top, on a shadowy lawn.
Plain in the dew her footsteps!

OLD MAN [Striking a lance through his side]
Dead!

HE [Gasping]
Immortal
Goddess! Wisdom! Face o' Night! Beyond the twilight bars

[**HE** dies.

OLD MAN [Striking the spear through him again]
Cast stones!

THE GIRLS [To the **MEN**]
Cast stones!

[They gather stones in their skirts and drop them in great number on to the body, until it has the resemblance of a cairn. Whilst they hurry about the **OLD MAN** speaks to any that will listen to him.

For that this was a Prince raise him a tomb,
Casting your stones on it. In sun nor gloom
Come never here again Here shall be moans
And whisperings of blasphemy to hear were doom
Cast there, stones there, above his lips that lied.
So be his name forgotten Never a word
From henceforth of his dying. This true lance
That slew him shall be burnt. . . . Never a word,
Never a word of him again But dance,
Choose a new mate for Lalagé's soft side
This night. Yes there, above his lips that lied.

[They begin to disperse.

A YOUNG GIRL
I would he had kissed me ere he died.

OLD MAN [Shaking his head misgivingly, to another **OLD MAN**.
You heard?

[They all go away over the plain in **GROUPS** of two and three; the poplars and the ruined temple have disappeared into the last light: the white garments have blue and purple shadows and the evening star shakes out brilliant rays in the dusky sky.

THE VOICE OF A YOUNG GIRL [singing in the distance]
When he comes from seawards,
When he comes from townwards,
My love sings to me words
That my heart Hkes well.

[The night wind sweeps down; the watch-fires at the foot of the hills spring up as if they had been replenished and waver along the wind. It reaches the cairn of stones and runs with a sifting sound among the dry grasses around. It continues through the night.

A MASQUE OF THE TIMES O' DAY

(A FRAGMENT)

The Persons of the Masque:
The **DAWN** that shall wear a saffron gown, and in her hair daffodils.
HIGH NOON that shall wear a golden dress and necklets of amber.
EVENTIDE that shall be habited in grey and have glow-worms on her brow.
Night that shall be dressed in black zvith a coronal of stars and the crescent moon.

The Scene shall be a hilltop, high in air, with the blue sky painted fair on the backcloths. There shall be a great gilt framework Sphere of the Universe, set with jewels for the stars, and with the Signs of the Zodiac.

It shall revolve slowly, and within shall sit the **DAWN**, **HIGH NOON** and **OTHERS**. In its centre there shall be a great Globe of the Earth with the lands and the seas fairly marked. Round about it shall go **ONE SCORE** and **FOUR MEN** bearing the four-and-twenty torches of the Hours. Without, shall stand a **MAN** and a **WOMAN**.

A **CHORUS** habited like a reverend old man shall enter and shall tell how that the Times of Day, being weary of long contentions for the Dominion of the earth, have set this **MAN** and this **WOMAN** to choose which of these four shall have sole Empire.

The Music shall sound, and when it shall have ceased, the **DAWN** shall step forth from the Sphere as it revolves and shall say:

I am the Dawn, beloved by those that watch.

Then **HIGH NOON**:
I am the Noon, beloved by those that toil.

Then **EVENTIDE**:
I am the Eve, beloved by those that tire.

Then **THE NIGHT**:
I am the Night beloved by them that love.

Then shall those four dance together until the **DAWN** stands forth from among them and sings:

I am the Dawn, beloved by those that watch,
I come a-creeping, I come a-stealing
Over eastern mountains, over dewy lawns,
Pale, golden, slender, pale and very tender.
Unto you who've watched the night through hoping for the dawn's
Rise to usher Hope back.

[A dance again, and then **HIGH NOON** shall sing:

I am High Noon, beloved by those that toil.
I bring your resting times, ring your midday feasting chimes,
Pan's hour that brings youpantingto the hedgerows,
Dalliance in the river rushes,
In the shadows and deep hushes,
Over bee-filled beds of potherbs, over bird-filled, quivering woodlands.
Blessed rest in summer days, surcease 'neath the Summer haze.

[A dance again, and in her turn the **EVENTIDE** shall sing:

I am the Eve, beloved by those that tire.
All along the sunken lanes
And across the parching plains
I set dewy winds a-blowing,
Bring the cattle byrewards, lowing;
Bring the bats out, lure the owls out, lure the twilight beasts and fowls out;
Bid a broadening path of moonbeams hunt the homing smacks from seaward,
Flitting past the harbour lanthorns, trailing in a flight to leeward;
Set the harbour tumult rounding up the misty windings of the mountains;
Set my tiny horns a-sounding by the rillets, by the woodland fountains . . .
Tiny, tiny gnat-horns sounding in an intermitting cadence,
Cry, " Stroll homewards men and maidens,
Done is done and over's over.
Leave the wheatfields, quit the clover.
Masters, hired ones, all you tired ones,
Troop along the dog-rose lanes, troop across the misty plains,
Done is done ... is done, and over's over."

The **NIGHT** shall step forward and shall catch at the arm of the **EVE**. Then shall **NIGHT** say:

[To the **EVE**]
Enough, enough,
You steal too many of my silent hours . . .
[To the **MAN** and the **WOMAN**]
I am the Night beloved by them that love
As you do love.

I am that Night
That was in the beginning, I am she
That shall be the end . . . You come from me
And hasten back to me, and all the rest
Is shadow.
What's the Dawn?
The shadow of a dream . . . And what High Noon?
A vague unrest, a shadow on your slumbers . . .
And Ung'ring Eve has shadows in her hair,
The shadows of a shadow She's a thief
That steals my attributes, and is beloved
Because she is my shadow.

I am Truth,
A darkness, a soft darkness. And in that
Is all that's worth the seeing. In my arms
Is all that's worth the having. I'm august
But tender . . . tender . . . Oh, you mortal things,
That pass from Night to Night, from womb to womb
I am the best.

[She sings.

Over my grasses go, for a little while
I'll bid my flowers breathe their faint night scents.
For a little while
Go close together, straining lip to lip,
Go close together, straining heart to heart.
For a little while . . . for all the time you have.

[She speaks again.

The soft warm darkness shall hang overhead,
The great white planets wheel from the horizon.
You shall not know the nakedness of shame,
Nor know at all of sorrow on the earth,
The while I hang above you with the face
Of a wan mother, white with light of stars.

[She sings again.

Over my grasses go for a little while.
Hearing no sound, seeing no sight of earth,
For a little while

Cling close together, straining lip to lip,
Cling close together, straining breast to breast,
For a little while ... for all the time you have . . .

[She speaks very low, as if to herself.

And at the last
A wind shall sigh among my whispering grasses,
The planets fail behind a brooding cloud,
Your eyelids shall fall down upon your eyes
And it shall be the end . . .

[She sings as if triumphantly.

Under my grasses lie for the rest of time.
Hearing no sound, thinking no thought of earth.
For the rest of time.
Lie close together, silent, ear to ear.
Lie close together, slumb'ring hand in hand.
For the rest of time, for all the time you have.

Then shall men unseen in the roof of the hall hoist out of sight the gilt Sphere of the Zodiac, and
there shall he disclosed a great globe of the Earth which had been hid within the other. Then shall
the four Times of Day Dance a solemn measure round the globe to the sound of music. There shall
be sundry devices. As that, there shall come a Woman called the Autumn habited in russet and
garlanded with streamers of berries of the hawthorn. And this Autumn would have the Times of Day
observe a nice distance, equal one from the other, and a flight of the birds called starlings shall be
set free. Then shall a reverend man dressed in furs, and bearing a heavy burden of thorns cut faggot
wise, enter. He shall he the Winter, and shall dispute with the Autumn as to the manner of the
dance. He shall wish the **DAWN** and the **EVE** to stand nearer **HIGH NOON**. And he shall prevail, and a
flight of great wood doves shall cross the hall. And in like manner shall come the Spring and the
Summer each with their due attributes. These last four shall join hands and dance round about the
Times of Day. Then shall come men to the number of the cycles that have passed since the year of
our Lord's birth, and shall dance a solemn measure round them all. And a salvo of musquetoons shall
he shot off without, beneath the windows of the hall. And when the dance is ended
The End Piece shall be sung—

What if we say:
"These too shall pass away."
Whether we say it
Now, or delay it
How we may,
These too shall pass away.

THE WIND'S QUEST

Oh, where shall I find rest? "
Sighed the Wind from the west;
"I've sought in vain o'er dale and down,

Through tangled woodland, tarn and town,
But found no rest."

"Rest thou ne'er shalt find . . ."
Answered Love to the Wind;
"For thou and I, and the great grey sea
May never rest till Eternity
Its end shall find."

Note.—These lines, the first I ever wrote, were printed in the Anarchist journal, The Torch, in 1891.

Ford Madox Ford – A Short Biography

Ford Madox Ford was born Ford Hermann Hueffer on 17th December 1873 in Wimbledon, London, England, to Catherine Madox Brown and Francis Hueffer.   He was the eldest of three. His father, who became the music critic for The Times, was German and his mother English. He was named after his maternal grandfather, the Pre-Raphaelite painter Ford Madox Brown.

In 1889, after the death of his father, Ford and his brother, Oliver, went to live with their grandfather in London.

Ford later graduated from the University College School in London, but never went on to attend university.

In 1894, Ford eloped with his girlfriend from school Elsie Martindale. The couple were married in Gloucester and moved to Bonnington. By 1901, they had moved on to Winchelsea with their two daughters, Christina (1897) and Katharine (1900). Ford's neighbors in Winchelsea included the authors Henry James and H.G. Wells.

Ford collaborated with Joseph Conrad on three novels; The Inheritors (1901), Romance (1903) and The Nature of a Crime (published in 1924 but written much earlier). Ford would later complain that with Conrad, and indeed all his collaborators, his contribution was overshadowed by theirs.

In 1904, Ford suffered an agoraphobic breakdown due to increasing financial and marital problems. He travelled to Germany to spend time with family there and undergo treatment.

Among Ford's classic works are The Fifth Queen trilogy (1906–1908). These were historical novels based on the life of Catherine Howard, which Conrad, at the time, called 'the swan song of historical romance.'

In 1908, Ford founded The English Review. Within its pages he published works by and promoted the careers of Thomas Hardy, H. G. Wells, Joseph Conrad, Henry James, May Sinclair, John Galsworthy and William Butler Yeats; and debuted works by Ezra Pound, Wyndham Lewis, D. H. Lawrence and Norman Douglas.

Ford also wrote some outstanding poetry during his career. In the early decades of the century Ezra Pound and other Modernist poets in London valued his poetry for its treatment of modern subjects in contemporary diction as they sought to gain traction for their ideas.

Perhaps his most well-known work is The Good Soldier which was published in 1915. The story is set just before the carnage of WWI and narrates the tragic expatriate lives of both a British and an American couple using intricate flashbacks.

Ford was involved in British war propaganda as World War I ferociously unfolded across Europe. Among his colleagues were Arnold Bennett, G. K. Chesterton, John Galsworthy, Hilaire Belloc and Gilbert Murray. In his time there he wrote two propaganda books; When Blood is Their Argument: An Analysis of Prussian Culture (1915), with the help of Richard Aldington, and Between St Dennis and St George: A Sketch of Three Civilizations (1915).

Shortly after finishing the books he decided to enlist for the front line. He was 41 but accepted into the Welch Regiment on 30th July 1915.

Ford's poem Antwerp (1915) was praised by T.S. Eliot as "the only good poem I have met with on the subject of the war".

Ford's experiences both on the front line in France and his previous propaganda activities provided rich seams of experience for his later four volume work Parade's End, set before, during and after World War I in England and the Front line.

Ford had used the name of Ford Madox Hueffer, but, after World War I, thinking it sounded too Germanic and a probable hinderance to his career, changed it to Ford Madox Ford in 1919.

Romantic complications for Ford were something of a speciality and during his life he embarked on several affairs. Between 1918 and 1927 he lived with Stella Bowen, an Australian artist twenty years his junior. In 1920 they had a daughter together, Julia Madox Ford.

In 1924, he founded The Transatlantic Review, a journal with great influence on modern literature. Staying with the artistic community in the Latin Quarter of Paris, Ford befriended James Joyce, Ernest Hemingway, Gertrude Stein, Ezra Pound and Jean Rhys, all of whom he would publish.

Jean Rhys was initially of interest to Ford because, as she was born in the West Indies, she had, he declared, 'a terrifying insight and ... passion for stating the case of the underdog, she has let her pen loose on the Left Banks of the Old World'. It was also Ford who said she should change her name from Ella Williams to Jean Rhys.

At the time her husband was in jail for what Rhys described as 'currency irregularities' and so it seemed perfectly reasonable that she move in with Ford and Stella. In such close proximity they began an affair which would later end acrimoniously.

In Hemingway's Parisian memoir A Moveable Feast he describes a meeting with Ford at a café in the early 1920s. His description of Ford; 'as upright as an ambulatory, well clothed, up-ended hogshead.'

In reviewing his collaboration with Joseph Conrad, Ford said 'he disowns me now that he has become better known than I am. I helped Joseph Conrad, I helped Hemingway. I helped a dozen, a score of writers, and many of them have beaten me. I'm now an old man and I'll die without making a name like Hemingway.' At this Ford began to sob. Then he began to cry.

In the summer of 1927, Ford had moved to Avignon in France to convert a mill into both a home and a workshop. He called it 'Le Vieux Moulin'.

In 1929, he published The English Novel: From the Earliest Days to the Death of Joseph Conrad, a brisk and accessible overview of the history of English novels.

Ford spent the last years of his life teaching at Olivet College in Olivet, Michigan.

During his career Ford wrote dozens of novels as well as essays, poetry, memoirs and literary criticism. But as he himself said his works were overshadowed by those who found fame an easier friend. Today he is well-regarded but known only for a few works rather than the grand arc of his career.

Ford Madox Ford died on 26th June 1939 at Deauville, France at the age of 65.

Ford Madox Ford – A Concise Bibliography

The Shifting of the Fire, as H. Ford Hueffer (1892)
The Brown Owl, as H. Ford Hueffer (1892)
The Queen Who Flew: A Fairy Tale (1894)
The Cinque Ports (1900)
The Inheritors: An Extravagant Story, Joseph Conrad and Ford M. Hueffer (1901)
Rossetti (1902)
Romance, Joseph Conrad and Ford M. (1903)
The Benefactor (1905)
The Soul of London (1905)
The Heart of the Country (1906)
The Fifth Queen (Part One of The Fifth Queen trilogy) (1906)
Privy Seal (Part Two of The Fifth Queen trilogy) (1907)
An English Girl (1907)
The Fifth Queen Crowned (Part Three of The Fifth Queen trilogy) (1908)
Mr Apollo (1908)
The Half Moon (1909)
A Call (1910)
The Portrait (1910)
The Critical Attitude, as Ford Madox Hueffer (1911)
The Simple Life Limited, as Daniel Chaucer (1911)
Ladies Whose Bright Eyes (1911) (extensively revised in 1935)
The Panel (1912)
The New Humpty Dumpty, as Daniel Chaucer (1912)
Henry James (1913)
Mr Fleight (1913)
The Young Lovell (1913)
Antwerp (eight-page poem) (1915)
Henry James, A Critical Study (1915).
Between St Dennis and St George (1915)
The Good Soldier (1915)
Zeppelin Nights, with Violet Hunt (1915)
The Marsden Case (1923)
Women and Men (1923)
Mr Bosphorous (1923)
The Nature of a Crime, with Joseph Conrad (1924)

Joseph Conrad, A Personal Remembrance (1924)
Some Do Not . . . (1924)
No More Parades (1925)
A Man Could Stand Up (1926)
A Mirror To France (1926)
New York is Not America (1927)
New York Essays, Rudge (1927)
New Poems (1927)
Last Post (1928)
A Little Less Than Gods (1928)
No Enemy (1929)
The English Novel: From the Earliest Days to the Death of Joseph Conrad (One Hour Series) (1929)
The English Novel (1930)
Return to Yesterday (1932)
When the Wicked Man (1932)
The Rash Act (1933)
It Was the Nightingale (1933)
Henry for Hugh (1934)
Provence, Unwin, 1935.
Ladies Whose Bright Eyes (revised version) (1935)
Portraits from Life: Memories and Criticism of Henry James, Joseph Conrad, Thomas Hardy, H.G. Wells, Stephen Crane, D.H. Lawrence, John Galsworthy, Ivan Turgenev, W.H. Hudson, Theodore Dreiser, A.C. Swinburne (1937)
Great Trade Route (1937)
Vive Le Roy (1937)
The March of Literature (1938)

www.ingramcontent.com/pod-product-compliance
Lightning Source LLC
Chambersburg PA
CBHW060100050426
42448CB00011B/2547